Theory Workbook

Level Three

By Wesley Schaum

Schaum's Pathway to Musicianship

The *Schaum Making Music Piano Library* integrates method, theory, technic and note reading with appealing materials for recital and repertoire. Schaum's well-proven motivational philosophy and sound pedagogy are widely recognized.

FOREWORD

This workbook presents basic music theory intended to supplement any Level Three method book and for <u>all ages</u>. Recognition of accompaniment patterns, melodic patterns, and broken chords are emphasized because of their importance for note reading. The student is thereby encouraged to look ahead while reading and trained to read music analytically. The scale fundamentals presented here lay the groundwork for more analytical study of scales later. <u>Scale fingerings</u> for both hands are shown separately on the back inside cover.

For most students, one workbook page can be assigned every week; in some cases two pages can be assigned together. These pages should be checked and corrected <u>before</u> the "keyboard assignment" is started. Regular <u>keyboard practice of these workbook pages is essential</u> to reinforce the learning process.

INDEX

Schaum Publications, Inc.
10235 N. Port Washington Rd. • Mequon WI 53092
www.schaumpiano.net

02-83

Lesson 1: Repeat Signs

Name_____ Date_____ Score_____

Two dots in the center of the staff just before a double bar are called a *repeat sign*. It means to go back to the beginning and play once again. After playing the repeat section the second time, continue beyond the repeat sign. The line above the staff with arrows at each end shows the section to be repeated.

DIRECTIONS: Draw a line with arrows at both ends (as shown in the sample) above the measures repeated in each line below.

Repeat signs are often used in *pairs*. Repeat dots on the *right* side of a double bar show the *start* of the repeat section; repeat dots on the *left* side of a double bar show the *end*. The repeat section is shown by a line with arrows at both ends.

DIRECTIONS: Draw a line with arrows at both ends (as shown in the sample) above the measures repeated in each line below.

KEYBOARD ASSIGNMENT: After completing the written work, play each line, repeating the measures indicated with repeat signs. Do this at least three times per day.

Lesson 2: Consecutive Repeats and First & Second Endings

Name _____ Date _____ Score _____

Repeat sections may sometimes be next to each other. This results in repeat dots being on *both sides* of a double bar, as shown between measures 2 and 3, below. In the sample, the first two measures are to be played *two times*, then the last four measures are also to be played *two times*.

DIRECTIONS: Draw a line with arrows at both ends above each group of repeated measures in the two lines below.

First and second endings (see sample below) are used with repeat signs. The first ending is played only the *first time* in a repeat section; the second ending is played only the *second time*. Remember, when playing the *second* time of a repeat section the measures marked "1" are to be *omitted* and the measures marked "2" are to be played instead.

First and second endings may be one or more measures long and may occur anywhere in the middle of a piece or at the end of a piece.

DIRECTIONS: Draw a circle around the *first* endings below.

KEYBOARD ASSIGNMENT: After completing the written work, play each line, repeating the measures indicated and using the first and second endings. Do this at least three times per day.

Lesson 3: Octave Higher and Lower Signs

Name_____ Date_____ Score_____

The number **8** followed by a dotted line, placed **over** a series of notes, means to play **one octave higher** than written. The same symbol, when placed **under** a series of notes, means to play **one octave lower**. For a single note or chord there is often no dotted line. Instead, the symbol **8va** or **8vb** may be used. Octave signs affect only the notes in *one staff* (the staff closest to the sign).

Play One Octave Higher

Play One Octave Lower

The number **15** (sometimes **16**) followed by a dotted line means to play **two octaves higher or lower**. For a single note or chord, **15ma** = two octave higher, **15mb** = two octaves lower.

DIRECTIONS: Identify each octave sign by writing the correct abbreviation in the adjoining box.
1H = 1 octave Higher   2H = 2 octaves Higher   1L = 1 octave Lower   2L = 2 octaves Lower

Lesson 4: Changes of Clef

Name_____ Date_____ Score_____

DIRECTIONS: Draw a circle around all *clef changes* in each staff below. (You should find 16 clef changes.) Write the letter name in the box below each note. Consult the note chart on the front reference page if necessary.

KEYBOARD ASSIGNMENT: After completing the written work, play each line of music with the right hand; then play each line with the left hand.

Lesson 5: 8th Note Triplets

Name_____Date_____Score_____

A *triplet* is a group of three notes of equal value. They are played at a somewhat faster but very even tempo to fit into the same time-span as two normal notes of the same value. Triplets are usually indicated by a slur and an italic number 3.

* DIRECTIONS: Write the counting on the dotted lines below each measure. See Teacher's Note for choice of counting.

KEYBOARD ASSIGNMENT: After completing the written work, play each line of music; count aloud while playing. The first note of each triplet should get a small accent. Do this at least three times per day.

*TEACHERS NOTE: Because of different ways of teaching, the counting of triplet groups has purposely been left to the preference of the teacher. As a suggestion, you could use: "one-lah-lee," "two-lah-lee," etc. or "one-trip-let," "two-trip-let," etc. (the spoken number, of course, would depend upon the number of the beat). Saying a three syllable word such as "trip-oh-let," "beau-ti-ful," or "choc-o-late" often helps the student to feel the triplet rhythm.

Lesson 6: More 8th Note Triplets

Name_____ Date_____ Score_____

DIRECTIONS: Write the counting on the dotted lines below each measure.

KEYBOARD ASSIGNMENT: After completing the written work, play each line of music; count aloud while playing. The first note of each triplet should get a small accent. Do this at least three times per day.

Lesson 7: Recognizing Two Different Accompaniment Patterns

Name_____ Date_____ Score_____

DIRECTIONS: The first two measures of each of the following accompaniments are numbered with a bracket above. Compare these numbered measures with each measure in the remainder of the accompaniment. Draw a bracket and number "1" above measures which match the first pattern; draw a bracket and number "2" above measures which match the second pattern. In matching measures the notes and rhythm must be the same. Leave the space blank above any measure which is not an exact match.

KEYBOARD ASSIGNMENT: After completing the written work, play the notes in each measure. Do this at least three times per day.

TEACHERS NOTE: Recognition of patterns is a basic concept helpful in memorizing and later in analysis of musical form.

Lesson 8: Recognizing Three Different Accompaniment Patterns

Name_____Date_____Score_____

DIRECTIONS: Three measures in each of the following accompaniments are numbered with a bracket above. Compare these numbered measures with each measure in the remainder of the accompaniment. Draw a bracket and number "1" above measures which match the first pattern; draw a bracket and number '2" above measures which match the second pattern; draw a bracket and number "3" above measures which match the third pattern. Watch carefully; some measures will not match any of the three patterns. Leave the space blank above measures which do not match exactly.

KEYBOARD ASSIGNMENT: After completing the written work, play the notes in each measure. Do this at least three times per day.

Lesson 9: Metronome Marks

Name_____ Date_____ Score_____

The letters, *M.M., followed by a small note and number placed at the beginning of a piece or section of music are called a *metronome mark*. It specifies the speed or tempo of the music shown by a *metronome* indicating beats per minute. The higher the number the faster the metronome speed. The small note represents the note value in the music which gets *one beat* (one "click" of the metronome).

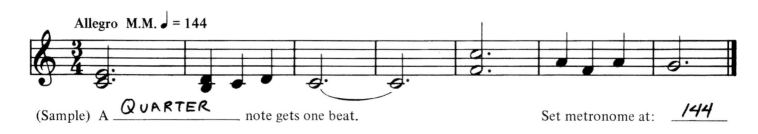

(Sample) A ___QUARTER___ note gets one beat.   Set metronome at: ___144___

DIRECTIONS: Name the type of note which gets one beat on the blank line below each staff of music. Then write the number at which a metronome should be set to give the correct beats per minute. The line above is a sample. The note that gets one *beat* ("click" of the metronome) does not necessarily get one *count*.

An _____ note gets one beat.   Set metronome at:_____

A _____ note gets one beat.   Set metronome at: _____

An _____ note gets one beat.   Set metronome at: _____

OPTIONAL KEYBOARD ASSIGNMENT: (Only if you have a metronome at home.)
After completing the written work, set your metronome to the speed shown in the first metronome mark. Start the metronome and play the notes in the first group of measures at the proper speed. Then do the same for the other groups of measures on the page.

* The original mechanical metronome was invented in 1815 by J.N. Maelzel, therefore the abbreviation, M.M. (Maelzel's metronome).

Lesson 10: Major Scale Construction: E Major

Name_____ Date_____ Score_____

The MAJOR SCALE is a pattern of *whole steps* and *half steps* in musical alphabet order. The eight notes of the major scale have number names called *degrees*. The keyboard shows the *C Major Scale* with degree numbers printed below each letter. The two *Half Steps* are indicated by a slur and the letter H. All other steps are *Whole Steps*.

Remember that in *any* major scale the half steps are always between the 3rd-4th and 7th-8th degrees.

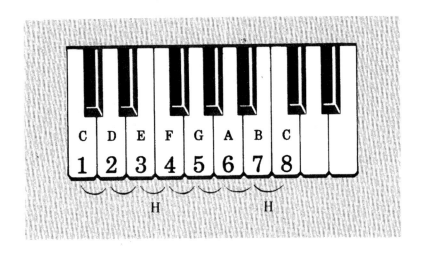

Notes of the *E Major Scale* are shown below with scale degree numbers. The letter H shows the location of the two *Half Steps*.

DIRECTIONS: Add sharps where necessary to make the pattern of *whole* steps and *half* steps for the *E Major Scale* in both staffs. Write letter names, including the correct sharp, in the box below each note.

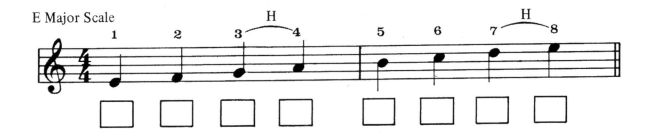

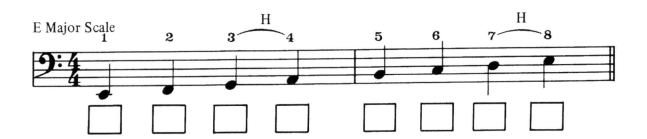

KEYBOARD ASSIGNMENT: After completing the written work, play the E Major scale with each hand, using the fingering shown on the back reference page. Do this at least three times per day.

TEACHERS NOTE: It is recommended that the student be *at the keyboard* when doing the written work on this page.

Lesson 11: Finding Roots of I, IV and V

Name_____Date_____Score_____

To help organize and analyze music, scale degrees are given Roman numerals and names to indicate the roots of chords. The three *primary* chords are:

Scale Degree	Roman Numeral	Name
1	I	Tonic
4	IV	Sub-dominant
5	V	Dominant

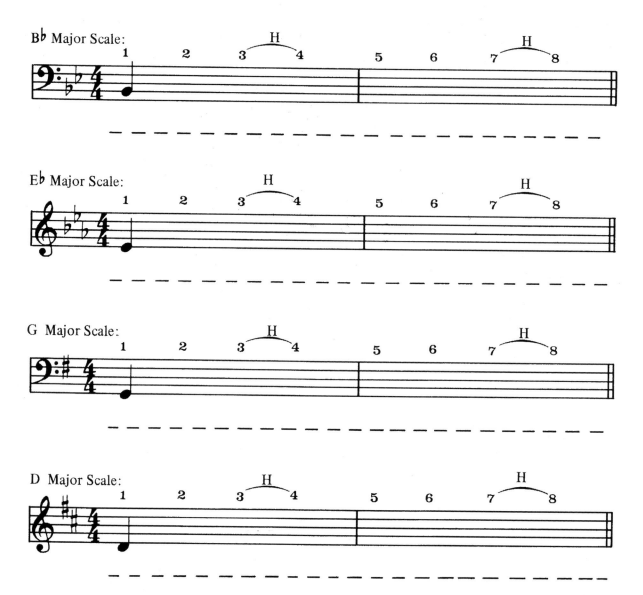

DIRECTIONS: Write the notes for each of the major scales shown below. The starting note of each scale is printed. Write Roman numerals I, IV and V on the dotted lined below the first, fourth and fifth degrees of each scale, as shown in the sample above.

KEYBOARD ASSIGNMENT: After completing the written work, play each line of music, saying the number I, IV or V aloud as these scale degrees are encountered. Do this at least three times per day.

Lesson 12: Building Major Triads: I, IV and V

Name _____ Date _____ Score _____

A *major triad* is a three-note chord using every-other scale degree *starting from the bottom note* called the *root*. Major triads are built on I, IV and V of any major scale. The C major scale is shown in the line below.

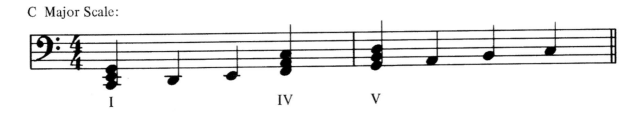

DIRECTIONS: Write the notes for the I, IV and V chords for each of the scales below. Add stems to all notes. Write the Roman numeral I, IV or V below the appropriate chords.

KEYBOARD ASSIGNMENT: After completing the written work, play the I, IV and V chords from each line of music. Do this at least three times per day.

Lesson 13: Recognizing Two Different Melodic Patterns

Name_____ Date _____ Score_____

DIRECTIONS: Compare the patterns in each measure of the melodies below; you will find two different patterns that are repeated several times in each melody (the first line is a sample). Draw a bracket and number "1" above the measures with the *first* pattern; draw a bracket and number "2" above the measures with the *second* pattern. In matching measures the notes and rhythm must be the same. Leave the space blank above any measures which are not an exact match.

KEYBOARD ASSIGNMENT: After completing the written work, play the notes in each measure. Do this at least three times per day.

Lesson 14: Recognizing Three Different Melodic Patterns

Name_____ Date _____ Score _____

DIRECTIONS: Compare the patterns in each measure of the melodies below; you will find three different patterns that are repeated several times in each melody (the first line is a sample). Draw a bracket and number "1" above the measures with the *first* pattern; draw a bracket and number "2" above the measures with the *second* pattern; draw a bracket and number "3" above the measures with the *third* pattern. Watch carefully; some measures will not match any of the three patterns. Leave the space blank above measures which do not match exactly.

KEYBOARD ASSIGNMENT: After completing the written work, play the notes in each measure. Do this at least three times per day.

Lesson 15: Transposing by Scale Degrees

Name_____Date_____Score_____

To transpose a melody means to play it in a *different key*, starting on a higher or lower note. When transposing, you use a different *key signature*, notes from a different *scale*, and a different *hand position*.

The first seven notes of the major scales of F, B-flat and E-flat are shown with their scale degree numbers. These will be used to help in transposing.

The first six measures of "America" are printed below in the key of *F Major*. Scale degree numbers have been written under each note.

Look for the *interval direction* (up or down) of the melody. Notice that in the sample melody the 7th degree is *below* the 1st degree.

DIRECTIONS: Write the scale degree numbers for "America" on the lines below each measure. Then write the *notes* for "America' in the key of *B-flat Major*. The starting note is printed. Watch for different note values (half, quarter, eighth, etc.). When transposing, the stem direction may change because of different note positions in the staff.

DIRECTIONS: Write the scale degree numbers for "America" on the lines below each measure. Then write the *notes* for "America" in the key of *E-flat Major*. The starting note is printed.

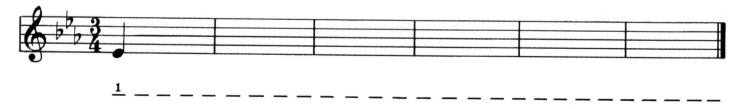

KEYBOARD ASSIGNMENT: After completing the written work, play "America" in all three keys. Do this at least three times per day. For an extra assignment, transpose "America" to the key of C Major (see keyboard diagram at top of Lesson 10).

Lesson 16: More Transposing by Scale Degrees

Name_____Date_____ Score_____

The first seven notes of the major scales of G, D and A are shown with their scale degree numbers. These will be used to help in transposing.

1 2 3 4 5 6 7   1 2 3 4 5 6 7   1 2 3 4 5 6 7

The first seven measures of "Lincoln and Liberty" are printed below in the key of *G Major*. Scale degree numbers have been written under each note. Look for the *interval direction* (up or down) of the melody. Notice that the 5th and 6th scale degrees are used in two places, above and below the *tonic* note (see Lesson 11).

5   1 1 1   3 2 1   3 5   6   5 3 2   1 2 3   6

DIRECTIONS: Write the scale degree numbers for "Lincoln and Liberty" on the lines below each measure. Then write the *notes* for "Lincoln and Liberty" in the key of *D Major*. The starting note is printed.

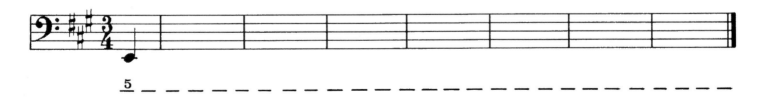

5 _

DIRECTIONS: Write the scale degree numbers for "Lincoln and Liberty" on the lines below each measure. Then write the *notes* for "Lincoln and Liberty" in the key of *A Major*. The starting note is printed.

5 _

KEYBOARD ASSIGNMENT: After completing the written work, play "Lincoln and Liberty" in all three keys. Do this at least three times per day. For an extra assignment, transpose "Lincoln and Liberty" to the key of F Major (see top of Lesson 15).

Lesson 17: Syncopated Rhythms

Name_____ Date_____ Score_____

Syncopation is a kind of rhythm with emphasis on a weak beat or between beats. Common forms of syncopated rhythms are an eighth-quarter-eighth-note pattern and tied notes. In the two sample lines that follow, there are brackets printed above the syncopated rhythms; the syncopated beats are circled. Syncopated rhythms are often found in ragtime, jazz, and most forms of popular music.

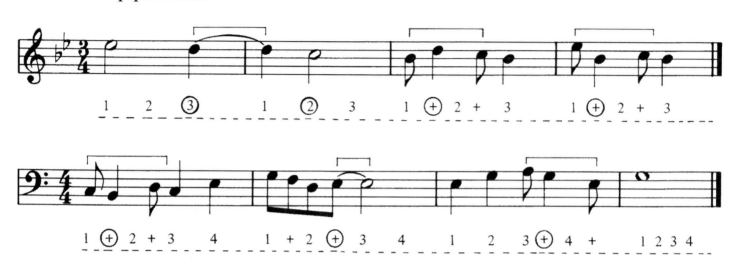

DIRECTIONS: Draw a bracket above each group of syncopated notes. Write the counting numbers on the dotted line below each measure. Then circle the beats where syncopated notes occur.

KEYBOARD ASSIGNMENT: After completing the written work, play all notes at the keyboard, giving a *small accent* to each note that is *syncopated*; count aloud as you play. Do this at least three times per day.

Lesson 18: Major Triads with Chord Symbols

Name_____Date_____Score_____

A *major triad* is built using the 1st, 3rd and 5th degrees of any major scale. The chord name comes from the bottom note, called the *root* (see Lessons 11 and 12). The chord symbol is the same as the name of the root. Any chord may be used in different octaves of the keyboard and written in different clefs.

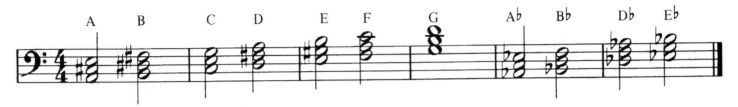

DIRECTIONS: Write the letter name of the *chord symbol* in the box above each chord. *Reminder*: a bar line cancels all accidentals from the previous measure.

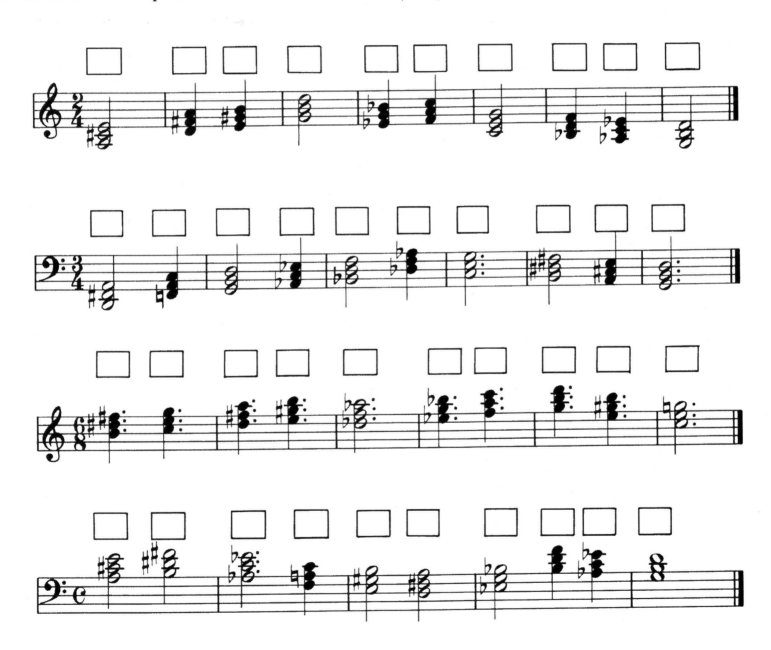

KEYBOARD ASSIGNMENT: After completing the written work, play the chords in each measure. Say the chord symbol name aloud as you play each chord. For extra practice play the chords one octave higher or one octave lower than written.

TEACHERS NOTE: This lesson and the one on chord next page are excellent opportunities for ear training. The student may be made aware of the *sound* of a *major triad* while playing the chords on these pages. Listening attentively while playing helps coordinate ear, eye, and finger training.

Lesson 19: Chord Reading with Key Signatures

Name_____ Date_____ Score_____

DIRECTIONS: Write the letter name of the *chord symbol* in the box above each chord. Watch for changes of key signature.

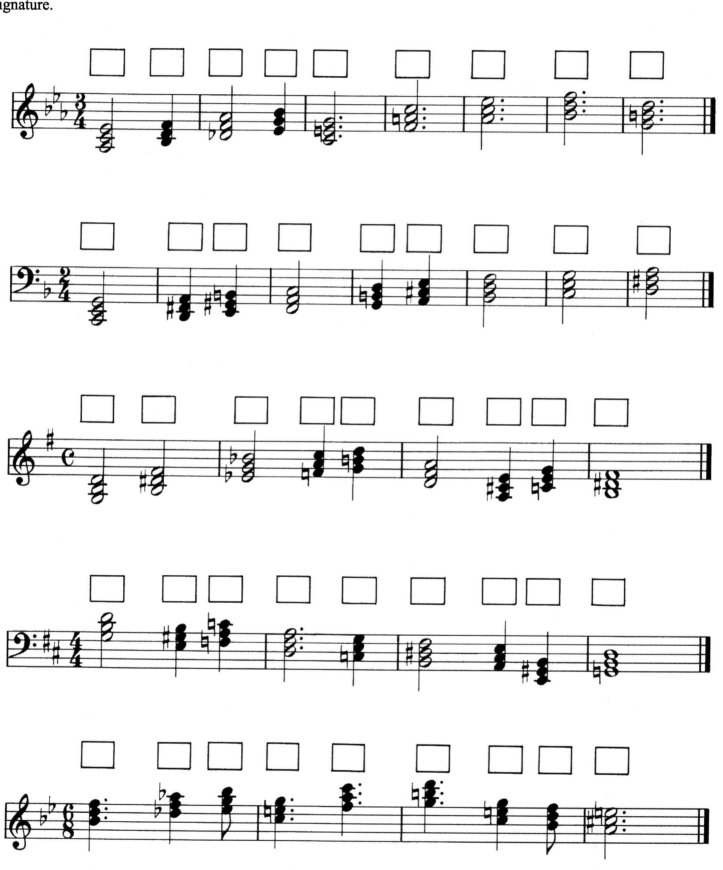

KEYBOARD ASSIGNMENT: After completing the written work, play the chords in each measure. Say the chord symbol name aloud as you play each chord. For extra practice, play each chord one octave higher or lower than written.

Lesson 20: Key Signature Changes

Name_____ Date_____ Score_____

A change of key signature is always preceded by a double bar. When necessary, one or more natural signs are used to cancel all or part of the previous key signature. The line below shows samples of three different key signature changes.

Key of B♭   Key of C   Key of G   Key of F   Key of E♭   Key of F

DIRECTIONS: Write the letter name of each key signature on the line above each measure. If necessary, refer to page 32 for key signature names.

Key of _____ Key of ____   Key of _____ Key of ____   Key of _____ Key of ____

Key of _____ Key of ____   Key of _____ Key of ____   Key of _____ Key of ____

Key of _____ Key of ____   Key of _____ Key of ____   Key of _____ Key of ____

Key of _____ Key of ____   Key of _____ Key of ____   Key of _____ Key of ____

TEACHER'S NOTE: It is assumed that all keys on this page are *major*. Minor keys will be explained in a later book of this series. If work on minor keys is wanted now, the Schaum *Scale Speller* is suggested.

Lesson 21: Recognizing Broken Chords from Triads

Name_____Date_____Score_____

The line below shows eleven different root position triads with chord symbols written above.

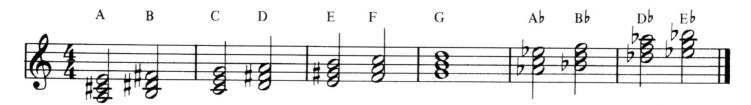

DIRECTIONS: Compare the broken chord in each measure with the triads at the top of this page. In the box above each measure, write the letter name of the triad from which the broken chord is made. Notice that some broken chords start from the bottom up; others start from the top down. The first two measures are samples.

KEYBOARD ASSIGNMENT: After completing the written work, play all measures at the keyboard. Say the chord letter name aloud as you play each measure.

Lesson 22: More Broken Chord Recognition

Name_____Date_____Score_____

DIRECTIONS: Compare the broken chord in each measure with the triads at the top of Lesson 21. In the box above each measure, write the letter name of the triad from which the broken chord is made. Notice that some measures have extra notes repeating part of the broken chord. The first three measures are samples.

KEYBOARD ASSIGNMENT: After completing the written work, play all measures at the keyboard. Say the chord letter name aloud as you play each measure.

Lesson 23: 8th Note Triplet Review

Name_____ Date_____ Score_____

DIRECTIONS: Write the counting on the dotted lines below each measure. Refer to Lessons 5 and 6, if necessary.

KEYBOARD ASSIGNMENT: After completing the written work, play each line of music; count aloud while playing. The first note of each triplet should get a small accent. Do this at least three times per day.

Lesson 24: Grace Notes: Melodic and Crushed

Name_____Date_____Score_____

A *grace note* is a small note played before the principal note (full size note). A grace note has *no time value* and does not affect the counting of the principal note. The principal note is played *on the beat*. A grace note may be above or below the principal note; see samples in the line below. A grace note is affected by a key signature and by previous accidentals in the same measure.

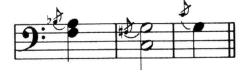

The *style, mood and tempo* of the music will determine the type of grace note:

MELODIC GRACE NOTE

TEMPO: *slow to medium*
STYLE or MOOD: *graceful, smooth, gentle, expressive, light, or delicate*

The grace note is played very quickly before the principal note. Both notes are played *separately* with an accent on the principal note. The grace note is slurred into the principal note.

CRUSHED GRACE NOTE

TEMPO: *fast to very fast*
STYLE or MOOD: *bold, strong, vigorous, playful, or rather heavy*

The grace note and principal note are struck together. The grace note is immediately released and the principal note is held for its full time value.

DIRECTIONS: Study the tempo mark and title for each melody excerpt below. Decide which grace notes are to be *melodic* or *crushed*. Draw a circle around all grace notes which are to be *crushed*. (Do not make any mark on *melodic* grace notes.)

KEYBOARD ASSIGNMENT: After completing the written work, play all measures at the keyboard using the correct style of grace note.

TEACHERS NOTE: At first, it is recommended that just these two basic interpretations of the grace note be taught. As the student becomes more advanced, additional fine points of the grace note may be added.

It is generally agreed that prior to and during Beethoven's time, the grace note was played *on the beat*. After Beethoven, the grace note was played *before the beat* (with the principal note played on the beat).

Lesson 25: 16th Notes in Various Time Signatures

Name_____ Date_____ Score_____

DIRECTIONS: Draw a circle around all the 16th notes in the staffs below. Write the counting on the dotted lines below every measure. The first line is a sample.

KEYBOARD ASSIGNMENT: After completing the written work, play each line of music; count aloud as you play. Do this at least three times per day.

Lesson 26: A-flat Major Scale and Key Signature Review

Name_____Date_____Score_____

Notes of the *A-flat Major Scale* are shown below with scale degree numbers. The letter H shows the location of the two *Half Steps*. If necessary, refer to the explanation of major scales in Lesson 10.

DIRECTIONS: Add flats where necessary to make the pattern of *whole* steps and *half* steps for the *A-flat Major Scale* in both staffs. Write letter names, including the necessary flat, in the box below each note.

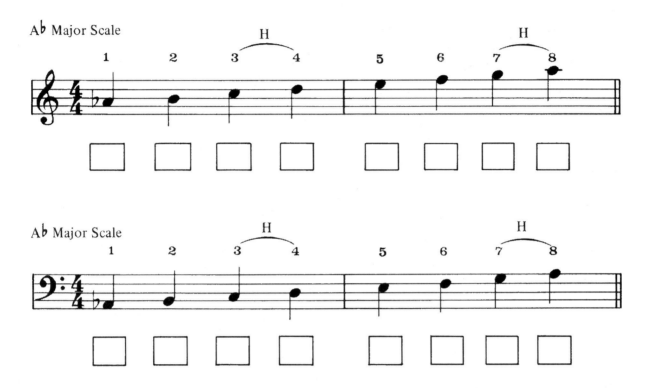

DIRECTIONS: Write the letter name of the key on the line below each measure. If necessary, refer to page 32.

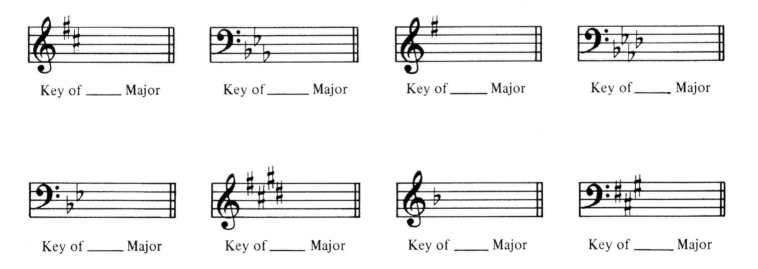

Key of _____ Major

Key of _____ Major

Key of _____ Major

Key of _____ Major

Key of _____ Major

Key of _____ Major

Key of _____ Major

Key of _____ Major

KEYBOARD ASSIGNMENT: After completing the written work, play the A-flat Major scale with each hand using the fingering shown on page 32. Do this at least three times per day.

TEACHERS NOTE: It is recommended that the student be *at the keyboard* when doing the written work on this page.

Lesson 27: Musical Form

Name_____ Date_____ Score_____

Composers plan their music with an outline called a *form*. Letters are used to represent the sections in a piece of music. These sections, called "themes," are usually from four to thirty-two measures long. Simple pieces have short themes, advanced pieces usually have longer themes. Examples of common musical forms can be outlined as:

A - B - A   A - A - B - A   A - B - A - B.

The notes in sections labeled "A" may vary a little. For example, the second "A" might be one octave higher than the first; or the second "A" might have a few notes of melody or accompaniment changed. If so, it is labeled "A^1" or "alternate A."

KEYBOARD ASSIGNMENT: The four lines of music below are labeled A, A^1, B and C. At the keyboard, play these lines of music in each of the following combinations to illustrate different musical forms.

1. A - B - A   4. A - B - A - B   (optional:)

2. A - A - B - A   5. A - B - C - A^1 7. A - B - A^1

3. A - A^1 - B - B   6. A - B - A^1 - C - A   8. A - A^1 - B - A

Notice that two extra notes are added to line "A^1." Otherwise, "A^1 " is the same as line "A."

TEACHER'S NOTE: Knowing the musical form is a big help when *memorizing* a piece of music. Show the student how to identify the musical form in other pieces.

Lesson 28: Trills and 16th Note Refresher

Name_____Date_____Score_____

The *trill* is a musical ornament abbreviated by the letters "tr" usually followed by a wavy line. The *principal note* is the note directly below the trill symbol. The trill is performed by rapidly alternating the principal note and the note on the scale degree above. The interval between the trilled notes may be a half step or a whole step.

A common trill consists of 16th notes beginning with the principal note. The trill continues for the length of the principal note and any tied note. Notes of a trill are affected by the key signature and by previous accidentals in the same measure. The line below shows samples of two trill symbols and how they are played.

As a reminder, the line below shows three notes along with the number of 16th notes that fit in the same time space. This will be helpful in writing the trills on the lower half of this page.

DIRECTIONS: Write the notes for each trill as indicated by the trill symbols in each line. If necessary, refer to the top of Lessons 15 and 16 for major scale notes. Watch for changes of time signature.

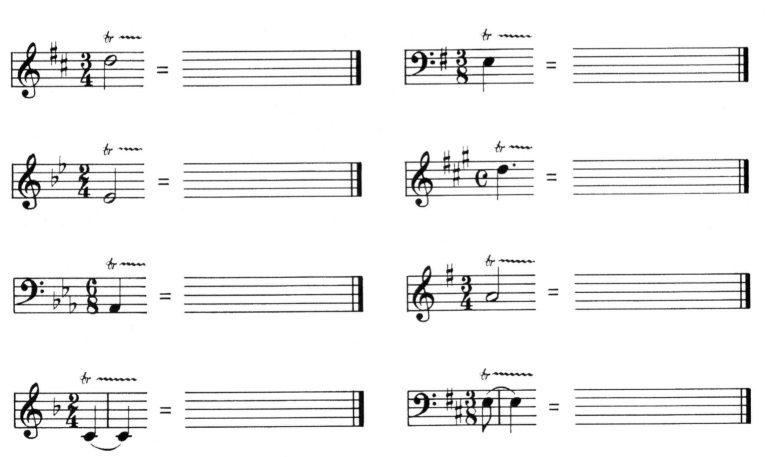

KEYBOARD ASSIGNMENT: After completing the written work, play each trill. Do this at least three times per day.

TEACHER'S NOTE: It is recommended that the student's first encounter be with a basic "measured" trill (equivalent to 16th notes) starting on the principal note, as shown here. Trills beginning on the *upper* note, as well as "improvised" or "free-style" trills may be presented at a later time as they are encountered in music of different styles and composers.

Lesson 29: Dotted 8th and 16th Notes

Name_____ Date_____ Score_____

A *dotted eighth* note is equal to one *eighth* note tied to a *sixteenth* note. The dotted eighth note is usually combined with a single 16th note. When connected by a beam, the 16th note has a short double beam, as shown in the line below.

A dotted 8th and 16th together make one beat in 2/4, 3/4 and 4/4 time, the same as a quarter note.

DIRECTIONS: Write the counting on the dotted lines below each measure. The first two measures are a sample.

KEYBOARD ASSIGNMENT: After completing the written work, play each line of music; count aloud while playing. Do this at least three times per day.

TEACHER'S NOTE: Because of different ways of teaching, the counting of the dotted 8th and 16th has been purposely left to the preference of the teacher. As a suggestion, you could use: "one-and-ah" ("ah" representing the 16th note) or "one-and-tee"; the spoken number, of course, would depend upon the number of the beat.

Lesson 30: More Dotted 8th and 16th Notes

Name_____ Date _____ Score _____

DIRECTIONS: Write the counting on the dotted lines below each measure. Refer to Lesson 29, if necessary. The first measure is a sample.

KEYBOARD ASSIGNMENT: After completing the written work, play each line of music; count aloud while playing. Do this at least three times per day.

Lesson 31: 9/8 Time Signature

Name_____Date_____Score_____

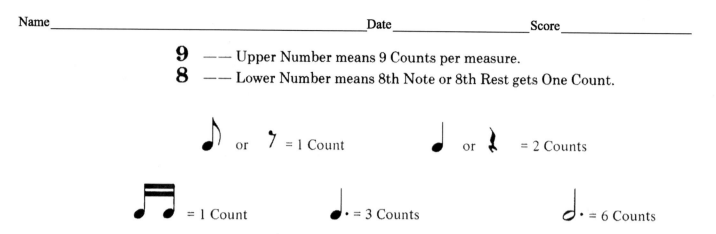

9 —— Upper Number means 9 Counts per measure.
8 —— Lower Number means 8th Note or 8th Rest gets One Count.

The note and rest values in 9/8 time shown above are the same as in 6/8 time.
The line below is a sample of counting in 9/8 time.

DIRECTIONS: Write the counting on the dotted lines below each measure.

KEYBOARD ASSIGNMENT: After completing the written work, play each line of music; count aloud while playing. Do this at least three times per day.

TEACHER'S NOTE: Counting in 9/8 time may be taught in groups of three (three counts per beat; three beats per measure) with a slight accent on counts 1, 4, and 7.